SETBACK
to
COMEBACK

A guide to live **YOUR** life

J A I

BlueRose ONE
Stories Matter

First Published in March 2022

ISBN: 978-93-93809-76-6

BLUEROSE PUBLISHERS

www.bluerosepublishers.com

info@bluerosepublishers.com

+91 8882 898 898

Cover Design:

Muskan Sachdeva

Typographic Design:

Ilma

Distributed by: BlueRose, Amazon, Flipkart

To my father and mother for everything.

Preface

On facing similar emotions again and again I decided to pen down my emotions at the instant I felt it and ended each poem with it's rectification steps as realized the moment I recovered from that low emotional state i.e. depression and recovery phases both are captured.

This book is a collection of poems which I wrote to help myself in bad times. And I revisit them to feel good, strong and motivated whenever I feel low due to any reason as almost all life's instances when one feels depressed or defeated is recorded. This way I saved a lot of my time and preserved much of my energy which were thus used in other constructive work.

Now it's available for the world to try all tested principles to save time and energy to be used in productive constructive work.

It took around a year to compile the entire poetry which initially written in bits and pieces was further composed, aligned and realigned. Taking much of time was unavoidable as diving into that emotional state where words would come from within wasn't easy

In a way readers will witness here live emotional state as felt by we humans expressed in words.

Acknowledgement

My sincere gratitude to my friend Nupur for motivating me to start writing and compiling them in a book to be useful for others.

To my friends Rashmi, Akanksha and many others and my sister, wife and other relatives for being such a reader that every writer aspires to have, which kept me motivated to compose one poetry after another.

To my parents, my wife and my sister for their patience, teachings and support which helped me to give birth to this life guide.

To Kashish for the beautiful sketches.

Introduction

This book is a compilation of lessons taught by life. It's an attempt to share the wisdom to enlighten path to one's dreams.

The lessons are organized in a crisp, modern and rhythmic verses so that it's easy to read, grasp and implement in one's life. At times real life examples are taken to make the teachings easy to understand.

This book is not for people who are pacified with whatever life brings to them. Rather this book is dedicated to all those people who want to lead a happy fulfilling life, to those who despite setbacks know to come back stronger, sharper and wiser. And if you're reading this then congratulations this book is for you.

Every possible situation which holds people back from accomplishing higher standards of personal and professional achievements are tried to be covered which can help people to prosper in every stage of life. Just don't read entire book at once, rather try to read relevant content only. And keep revisiting the book at moments you have negative feelings be it of anger, jealousy, hatred, loss, guilt, shame, doubt or defeat.

To live life happily without sacrificing any of goals be it family goals, society goals, professional goals or individual goals is the motive of every person born. This collection is made crisp and short so that it could be a handy guide for living a happy, energetic and fulfilled life.

At places I've used "He" owing it's usage recently to symbolize all human beings i.e. both men and women. Ladies are requested to please not take it otherwise.

Contents

To start with

I'm getting sick I'm getting insane
Is it self inflicted or is world giving me pain

I often sit and wonder.....
Why soft words are taken for leverage
Why backstabbing is praised rather than courage

Why shrewdness has become everyday's job
Why can't most break the trend of followers of mob

Why harsh and strong words get result faster
Why integrity is losing shine by success of backstabber

Why evil has so deep engrossed it's foot
Why is there even a need to prove truth

Why can't sorrow faces be bade bye bye
Why can't happiness never die

Why can't compassion be viral

Why can't hatred vanish as if surgical

Why do we have to think twice to trust

Why can't genuine friendship replace lust

Why bargaining with poor makes you feel grand

Why a lot of poor are humble than affluent

Why not to share before we consume

Why do we get demotivated very soon

I've tried to cover most reasons and answers in coming pages

Which if brought into practise is bound to increase your wages.

Start Living….

Way to live

Don't live to regret
Don't live to be said
Don't live to be afraid
"I'm enough", make sure it's being said

Don't die before you're dead
The dreams are not to be kept
Fear of losing is enough to be now left
Your bucket list, make sure it gets checked

Don't let your life be rented
Unfold your blanket
Unplug from their socket
Don't bother what they said.

One life is all you get
Play all the shots that's left
You receive the best when you least expect
Make sure "Try me" instead of "Why me" is being said.

On offer

Tored apart but will never betray
Offered few but I will ensure a full tray

Neglected but will take care
Snatched from but will offer my chair

Back-stabbed but will be considerate
Mocked but will not laugh at

Failed but will guide to win
Provoked but I teach calmness in any din

Stuck but will keep pulling you out
Discredited but will help to stand out from crowd

Lost but will show you the way
Haunted by but will ensure comfortable stay

Cried but will make you laugh
Opportunities missed but will guide to worth an autograph

Weakened but will make you strong
Am here to help to not be in sorrow for long

Thus I know a lot of things not to do
To guide you through what maximum don't have any clue.

Fear, an illusion, non-existent yet most powerful Dream snatcher.

Fear

Why I don't like myself when

Every time I see around things which I don't have

Every time I see those successes I crave

Every time I see those who are which I'll be

Every time I ponder over my dreams I see

Every time I am fed up seeing same face in mirror

Every time people congratulate me for what I don't see dear

Every time I get excited to start but soon end at midway

Every time I'm unable to do what heart say

Every time I'm feeling same after doing the same again

Every time I decide to quit status quo but then can't take a stand

Every time I'm motivated to do but soon comes demotivation

Every time I am about to move but then comes procrastination

Why is it so?

Is this due to Fear?

Fear of what's already there might not stay near

Fear of being embarrassed

Fear of being demotivated mid-way in the process

Fear of not being able to finish what I start

Fear of what people would think if I miss the dart

Fear of not being able to change

Fear of inability to catch up with what I dreamt

Fear of whether I'm losing a better option

Fear of not being able to stand up to other's expectation

Fear of dreaming too big as they say

Fear of distractions to come in my way

Fear of lack of self control

Fear of dying while on roll

Fear of falling in love again

Fear of being used for the same

Fear of not having found what I truly want

Fear of having one more failure to haunt

Fear of being tainted

Fear of not accomplishing what's expected

Fear of being down in the list

Fear of not acknowledging the gist

Fear of passive acceptance

Fear of repentance

Fear of being afraid

Fear of situations which demotivate

Fear of ending worse than present state

Fear of failure

Fear of repeating previous year

Fear of loosing dear

Fear of going too far from those near

Fear of not finding trusted peer

Fear of being unclear

Fear of getting rude

Fear of again unable to conclude

Fear of being unclear

Fear of fear

Take a moment……What exactly is this fear?

Wake up..watch around

Can fear kill or get you bound?

It can't so, it ain't physical neither any spirit in wind

It's just something that lives only in your mind

In your top-floor why is such a notorious creature allowed

How dare the unwelcome come in your house and shout

Isn't it about what might or could happen

Have you see the future? No-one has and will captain.

Don't let Fear leave all your dreams unfulfilled

Do what you Fear, it's sure to leave you thrilled

Even if you loose pursuing what fear says won't

You would be at a better place than if don't

Identify and empower fear by your determination to succeed

Fight it with courage to let so-called FEAR bleed.

With each master of their Sensible self,
World would be Enchanting shelf.

Master and Slave

You are not what your think you are

Rather you are what they
have made you think who you are

Feeding your subconscious according to
what they want to

Creating demands for their products that you never longed
for true

Buying what masters have been selling you so far

They make sure you don't stand at par

Being made a slave to the desires they create

You have been killing self by enlarging the
voids they made

Have been earning billions enticing you to earn millions

When this humanity is so much at stake

Dare to stand up and stand out from the crowd

Everyone is waiting for the other to shout

If they have done, you don't need to repeat it

You are on own mission, go and complete it

Go help that child, old, beggar and those alive

Rather than walking with candles or lamenting over what could be thrived

Masters have been exploiting
your desire to be anyhow happy

Need is to sooner get the gist though it's getting tricky

Be your own master, it's your life and you got to raise the stakes

Stand out, help yourself and others, let's make this world a beautiful place

You are an infinite being

Have all powers to fulfil your dream

Only if you start being your own master will you be in the cream.

Steering wheel of your Life is all yours,
Don't rent it out.

Take charge of your life

Start taking responsibility of whatever happens to you...
Your past choices are responsible for what you're today
As you didn't chose to hold distractions at bay

You chose to enjoy while the need was for hustle
You chose to curse while in your mind was the hurdle

You were looking for a perfect ambience to start
And thus you never even tried to grab your dream cart
Or even if you tried to fill it a bit
You didn't finished, yet seemed to quit
It remained undone and you got some reason as excuse
You were too busy NOT to realize
need of rewiring the fuse

Because everyone else around is doing the same
So you too didn't tried how not to be lame

You rather chose to blame the situation and people
Slowly getting lost in maze being gleeful

Realizing later it had worsened the situation

Then being hard to re-tune the station

Only to be left with self to blame

But blaming hasn't ever improved past

It's important to realize that it was only you in every cast

You could have chosen to walk the other way

You could have overruled the temptation to sway

You could have owned the situation and
worked to improve

If you start taking charge of life, all your orders will move

So own your life because it's been and
will always be on you.

A start won't end unless it's Consistent,
One step at a time gets aims Distant.

One step at a time

Bit by bit, step by step

All things can be done, just identify to break

Take first step, start to solve

The solution to next will soon begin to evolve

A cricket century wasn't contrived in one strike

Every run made contributed to that pride

The ball was even missed sometime

But hits continued to be made
with no future loss in mind

None waits for road to be cleared to start

We keep moving through crowd and reach our spot

To think every hurdle to be cleared to begin is foolish

Nothing will be conquered then so stop
making such wish

Hurdles are just another manifestation of your mind

It looks bigger from far

But keeps getting smaller as you reach closer
So don't let it hold you from behind

Divide your goals in steps, finish first to reach second
Finish each step, you're then sure to reach the end.

Dreams when are Fed up,
Either die or Show up.

A Knock

A knock at my door kept getting hard

At 3 am i was afraid to go as it was too dark

It didn't stopped so I had to take action

Called my security guard for inspection

The guy soon came with his weapon

Only to find no-one at the door

He thoroughly searched for any demon

Came back with a big NO & that my security is assured

The knock stopped for sometime

But while I was again going to sleep

A continuous louder knock this time

Wanted then to use my balcony for a leap

Chest throbbed, lungs felt hard to breathe

Throat went dry, eyes were afraid to weep

Was this a nightmare or a dream with opened eyes

Or was someone really desperate to hear my cries

I called the guard and asked again if he was sure

He said he was and will keep
having visits all night at my door

When knock didn't stopped I locked room and sat
wondering

I didn't wronged anyone nor I had any precious thing

Without any further heed I went to sleep

Next day I was wondering if it was to let
my life be tweaked

It could have been a ghost wanting to eat me live

Or it could be someone wanting to make me aware that I'm
alive

Did it wanted me to not accept the monotonous life I've

Or did it wanted me to not stop wishing the life I craved

Was it really at my external door

Or did unfulfilled dreams from inside were hungry and
roared

Did they were fed-up of being buried alive

I think I can't suppress them anymore, world will soon
witness them live.

Family quality Time is worth more than any Dime.

Relationship needs

We travel

We watch movies

We do shopping together

But do you know what's missing among one another

We laugh watching stand-ups

We wink in restaurants

We dance together

But haven't you felt something's missed altogether

We post updates

We take pictures

We enjoy food and music at get-togethers

But don't you think something's inside that bother

Don't you feel not being listened

Don't you feel you can't express own thoughts

Don't you feel being misunderstood

Don't you feel other don't care about your whereabout

Don't you feel there's much to talk about

Don't you feel to have peace around
Don't you feel to hold hands and just talk abound
Don't you feel to block all false attractions around
Don't you feel to be quiet and just gaze in huge amount

What exactly needed is........

Spend few hours of week talking with your loved ones
Stay from being parched by man-made glittering suns

Reflect on your relationships and work on them
Don't let busy schedule miss the gem

Focus on up-bringing of son and daughter
Don't take for granted mother and father

Learn to spend quality time and to laugh together
You need to fill the conversation gap before it's to bother.

Response to distraction determines
Winning or Losing.

Distractions

See around to find lots of things to grab
Lots of mesmerizing things ready to decorate our slab

Some are alive some make us feel alive
Temptations will be there to taste them live
Once acceptance given can't be taken back
Unless something gives us a whack

In seconds, strong web in mind can entangle
No productivity days then dangle
We'll want but not be able to say no
Can't feel anything but blue

Named as distractions these are eager to hug
Distractions of sex, smoking, alcohol and drug
Distractions of internet, food, other instant gratifications in life
Making us dance at tip of knife

Longer we stay with, more will be frustrated day

Better to pay heed and keep them at bay

Temptations can't tempt us against our wish

We can opt not to be lured by all this

Our decision is crucial being only chance on earth

Don’t keep handy anything without
even minuscule of dearth

Our stand separates loser from winner

Distractions are why similar soul’s status differ in success
ladder.

Wait…Look around,
People are happy with too less amount,
But wait, Observe what's abound,
Sad faces are more ample in count.

Happiness

Happiness is just a perspective to look at life :

Some are sad with a billion
Some can spread smiles possessing fraction of a million

Some are depressed with their job
Some spread happiness at every tick of clock

Some feel frustrated with life
Some take charge and get whatever they strive

Some frown at big things
Some thank even for small things

Some can't use opportunities
Some utilize even their adversities

Some feel grass being greener on the other side
Some sense blessing for every bite

Some keep aspiring for what others have
Some are satisfied with whatever little GOD gave

Some spend sleepless nights in mansion
Some take sound-sleep earning far from handsome

Some waste days pulling other's feet
Some feel alive winning leap after leap

Some have graves with no mark
Some make world dance at tunes of their harp.

Instant gratification is Chase of generation,
Pacifying falsely day to day frustration,
Wake up with habit of Meditation,
And welcome long lasting Exaltation.

Meditate

Does cigarette really relieves you of worries
And does alcohol really makes you forget memories

Do you want to fool self by forgetting problem
Does situation improves an inch from top to bottom
Then are those worth for the instant reliefs you get
Don't you want a long term solution to forget
To unlearn worries and your bad memories
And to learn to turn delicious any future bland curries

Let me guide you as to how to do so....

Sit comfortably
Close your eyes
Lighten your body
Take deep breaths
Let your thoughts come don't worry
Can't stop your thoughts but stop to give any fuck
Just let it flow like air in and out of your mind,
don't feel stuck

Focus on your breath, feel the ambience around

Think source of all happiness and
love engulfing you in amount

Bring smile at face, start to chant OM slowly

Visualize the symbol of OM wholly

Feel the air as you breathe gradually

You'll feel relaxed eventually

End with the feeling of blessing as white
light falling from above

Imagine it slowly covering your body like an envelope

Thanking higher power open your eyes &
spend day with love

This max 10 minutes process makes life happy as you want

Giving you reliefs from past and the strength to make
future grand.

LOVE,
For nothing's more favorite than Dove.

LOVE

Such a powerful thing this four letter word is
Is the sole reason to bring in world a bliss

When you learn to shower thing called love
Enemies are humbled by the action you shove
You then can handle tough things smoothly
Even jealousy can't stop you from being lively

Don't expect love unless you learn to give it for free
Learn from nature, recall sun and tree

Once you start to influence people's life with your deeds
It's too infectious to become victim of it's greed

It's the only slavery to willingly accept
Be so lovable that people just can't reject

Love for just your dear ones, Ahh!... it's now an old concept
Spread love for humanity, plants and animals i.e. in wider context

Love’s too powerful to solve what a fight can’t
Then universe forces conspire to give what you want

Don’t be remembered as someone who hates
It’s time when evil be shown the gates

Let's give the ill minded people a break
Spread love so much that harsh words feel at stake.

Take Life easy, Don't complex it out,
It's a Journey, Never a rout.

Feeling Lost

Has fear choked your throat
Is anger bleeding from eye
Are you wearing slaves coat
Has blue imbibed from sky

Is nose stuck of hatred
Are cheeks not getting red
Is sleep too busy to leave
Is mind too chasy to sleep

Did feet forget the path
Don't nature look smart

Have hands stopped to lend
Are fingers shy to command

Is head too heavy to think
Can't smile even blink

Is muscle too stiff

Has words stopped to click

Did breeze slapped

Why flowers look sad

Has Love been strange

Do season never seem to change

Is hair too messy

Is friends, family too cheesy

Even be it so, still...

Aren't you still alive?

Don't still mind belong to you?

Path to happiness isn't too complex to strive

For a start, feeling of gratitude for what's yours can do.

Detach darkness, exalt Sun.

Identify true people

I am thankful to all those people who said no
It's because of them I did alone
It's time to unsubscribe them from my show
I can now recognize who are welcome in home

Bringing me to witness hidden capabilities
Learning whom to rely in casualties
I thus learned to be independent
Whom my time should stop to pay rent
And who has been making in my life a dent.

It's better to get rid of leeches around
Before it devoids you of blood in abound

Huge amount is paid in the form of time and money
Isn't that precious enough to let not go awry
So I became choosey at the invitations I send
For who and who-not in my life should land
And made it a point in future to prevent

Any new weeds from infecting my life's plant
With which it can never become grand

A few helped to have my mess sorted
Let others regret what they have aborted

Let's make it a point to identify early The Cheats
Let only trustworthy occupy those luxury seats

Lessen your plates accordingly
Stop paying for extras uselessly
Let your life be then on a roll
With only those present who'll never get you bowled.

Marriages are said to be made in Heaven,
If last sweat ain't spend to save, it won't be Forgiven.

Marriage

Another lone coffee, another lone drink
Wonder if I'm filled with loneliness to the brink

Another cute girl another lovely smile
Sitting beside me catching my glimpse in a while

Finishing coffee hot, planned to sit for sometime
But waiter came for cup as there was waiting line

Other lone wolf's were also in queue to have the sip
Heard then voices to study marriage in deep
Was amazed as that's why was his India trip
Were mesmerized by Indian's long duration relationship

Foreigners wonder how two can stay together for so long
In my mind was then playing deception song
Song detailing grass to be greener on other side

Don't we feel uncomfortable when bonds are tied
Isn't now compromises for long being denied

Don’t after very few years our egos take stand

Growing divorce rates shows our pride can soon end

We'll repent what we had but ended on our own

Why the word compromise gets our mind blown

Is the journey alone comfortable thereafter

I have seen most loosing their laughter

Why can’t then adjustments be done to
make marriage last

Disadvantages maybe few but advantages are vast

Respect each other’s priorities, give other space

Clear misunderstandings, try to understand other’s case

Cherish love moments often for
admiration to fill any space.

Why double face?
Don't you fear Disgrace?

Twin personality

How can one switch personalities with such grace?

I wonder why people differ at back from at face

Who are you fooling around have you taken a heed

Change yourself else you'll be alone in need

May not initially but soon is exposed true face

Stop fooling yourself thinking to fool people always

Don't think no-one's smarter in your way

Might not complain but on chance people
will make you pay

Never can you find such soul's happy

Being in their social circle is too creepy

Not with friends, their company is of hypocrite souls

Who won't think twice to turn if other green signal glows

Such people end up with similar one's around

Deceiving self with dismay in abound

Don't you think straightforward people ever fell prey

Ever wondered why they so chose to stay

Reasons exist of people paying price for
honesty and integrity

To ensure no regrets while they're to finally be sleepy

But hypocrite ones are so busy mocking candid souls

Never realizing life slipping out of their controls

Being left speechless when honest
accomplish higher goals

Why don't they ever dare to rectify self's souls?

Time –handy yet most Valuable, free yet Priceless

Time

Time's too precious to let it go waste
Let your regret for past go in haste

Money gone can come back abound
But time can't be retrieved in any amount

Identify the culprits borrowing your time
Short term pleasures exploit like too much wine
It's your approval that's been given
Else they on own can't get you driven

You are wasting life by wasting time
You can change anytime the orders of dine

Sometimes it's hard to identify culprits
Need is to acutely take note in your mind chits
Else you'll end with no time for jobs worthwhile
While unworthy things will keep to beguile

Only when times all spent we recognize it's value

Wasting time is like decorating self's death-bed,
Let me warn you

" I was getting bored I was feeling alone

Unless a popup appeared on my phone "

Many such resources expend time

Some platters combination can poison dine

Sometimes we're so busy enjoying our past

That we don't realize our present running fast

Is time so much to let it go in vain

Don't we feel in past we should have taken pain

Don't we lament steps taken wishing it undone

Don't we wonder why we let time in past to run

All these didn't happened without your nod

Now stop shortening future line by any further knot

Get set, start to employ every second

Allot time to important jobs though by reckon

Make sure no moments go in waste

Your all orders will then be much delightful to taste

Life will change in such favorable ways

That you'll wonder why you were
missing such golden days.

Procrastination is habit of Loss,
For worthy to knowingly Loose toss.

Procrastination

We keep wondering that we have loads of time
Only to find out at last that we are late for dine

We have lots of things to do at first
That we unknowingly let important deeds to rust
This false sense of enjoyment
Is making in your life a dent

Leave your past it's gone
Don't bother for future it's not yet born
Nourish your present it's to be sown

It's better to finish before time than wait for the end
Else you'll realize need to take more time on rent
Which isn't ever gonna happen anyway
Stop procrastinating before life throws away

There isn't anything called on time
It's either before or after any deadline

Little success of past gets us so engrossed
That we forget there's lucky draw of future to toss
Thus the face upside is always of our loss
But we're satisfied that in past we were boss

Past is gone, future is yet to come
Need is to focus on now and get things done

Having too much time is a sham
If anyone says he won in last moment it's a scam
It was his attempt to finish task before time
That made him reach fast on the finishing line
Else unaccomplished will be the deadline

Time runs faster than one can realise
Stop wasting self and life and being unwise

Between you and dream before there's build a large crevice
Be brave and start to roll your dice
With that you'll even have one sixth chance to win
Else you'll be left with only to grin.

Discipline can achieve what others hadn't Expected,
Scaling heights that Dreams once accepted.

Discipline

Pursue Dream so hard that even nature
bends to fulfil demand

Do if hearts believes though mind says you can't

Do it aggressively with no brakes until the destination

Make it a routine as breathing in-out while respiration

One day undone slowly and slowly can take you far away

Slowly forgetting dream you'll slip to comfort zone

Your life will loose spark getting in monotonous tone

The tunes of a commoner will then start to play

You'll have to then force self to be gay

Soon you'll be hypnotized to take regular bend

However good a start is, you'll not reach desired end

Unless you make it a point to be disciplined

Unless you always ponder over what it meant

Unless you keep doing what it takes to get a step closer

Your dreams will keep looking farther and bigger

No-step taken will actually take you back

Forward steps will then slowly vanish from the map

Seeing another enrolment in commoner
they all will be glad

As another lost potential winner is what they'll have

There is a misconception of cool-of period

Which comes when pursuing goals you get stuck

And you feel to rely on luck

It's not when you haven't started anything yet

It's not when you feel burdened by the hurdles you get

So... get up tomorrow and make it a point

To devote every possible moment to the life you meant.

First step is Acceptance,
Next follows Correctance.

Accept it

Accept you're in pain

Accept that your life is lame

Accept there's need to improve

Accept it's time to groove

If you're infuriated take time to locate

Don't expect things to improve while you sat and ate

Be tough to yourself, start being harsh

Find ways to be in sun yet not be parched

Indifference or neglect isn't any solution at all

It'll slowly devoid the court of your ball

Seeing huge traffic you take alternate
route sooner to arrive

Why don't you do the same with life?

Huge traffic will delay you a lot

Stop pretending that things are fine, You're not a bot

Stop doing things to divert your disappointment

If you don't like, first need is it's acceptance

Then take corrective measures
instead of a later repentance

Identify the wrongs and start
working on them one by one

There's nothing of which mends can't be done

Don't be a tree with no option than
growing, giving fruits and dying

Take action now for the wrongs in your life and
stop lying

It's even better to be sad than fake with an ugly smile

You need to stop and take stock of wrongs
once in a while

Note down the wrongs and corresponding steps required

Get started, you need to be rewired

Else you'll miss this beautiful life a lot

Better is to cry now than when few moments before grave is
all you got.

Travel for hidden Potentials to unravel.

Travelling advantages

If you're in doubt and don't know what to do
If life gets you on edge where you can't get the clue
Pack your bags and go on travel
Your hidden potentials will then unravel

Watch the picturesque that's abundant around
See the greenery, mountain peaks and
pebbles that surround

Relax, take deep breaths and watch as birds flew
Don't use mobiles or camera, notice yourself getting new

Let your worries, anxieties and fear be blown by wind
Imagine in the vastness is burning all that had you bind

Learn from the things nature had to teach
Watch flower petals falling yet denying that soon end will
be reached

No matter how fast the wind blow
Or how strong the water flow

Even if temperature seems at all time low

No element can be seen in fear till death
snatches it's glow

There's a lot to embed in our life from this show...

Ever wondered why often our peace gets disturbed

Why can't we stand tall in adversities rather let dreams be robbed

Why we let overthinking terrify our laughter

Can't you witness both barren lands and green trees existing together

Why then in our society diverse opinions make people bother

Watch that desert and lonely pyramids also have fans

Every person has different capabilities, play it loud and dance

Choose not to be disturbed by turbulence around

You are sufficient and strong enough to break the chains that bound.

Ego lets happiness Go.

Ego

The world is so full of life and light
Why often people then want to cry
Don't they know none has shone bright
Unless their character gets to be light

What makes you feel you're above all
How long will little knowledge have you stand tall

Learn to shed your egos in and out
It kills more relationship than you doubt
From harming career in professional space
To getting personal life at times at stake

Why can't we move by taking all with us
Why accepting our mistake seem to be a fuss
Why can't we accept self being wrong
Is it jealousy or is hatred a thorn

Does accepting other to be right lowers your esteem

Or will it degrade your position in team

Won't you be more harmed when your wrong sweeps to surface

Isn't it better to be second than play foul and get disqualified in race?

Look into philanthropy's success to know whether ego works

Be vigilant of your ego if it often lurks

You can possibly fool others but not your own might

Isn't it better to make amends before chances get died?

Parents are God's incarnation on this earth.

Owe to parents

Do you really know who you are

Aren't you the product of those 2 dove

How and why did you start to hate

Was not your source only love?

Were you unlucky?

You are because of one in millions of sperms that fertilized an egg

Had either source changed, another person had been born having entirely different tag

Being given a chance to live is very big achievement

Celebrate this gift of life, try not to make any dent

You owe parents a lot, don't forget to bestow the Love's scent

They are the first deserving in front of whom to bent

Tiring days restless sleep

Exhausted yet relentlessly parents try for best child's upkeep

Difficult it is to upbring a child

But still they do it like they don't mind

Once the basics are given by parents

It's then up to you whether to convert to enticing scents

But today's children think they know more

They feel parents often get them bored

Didn't similar situations existed when we were child

Don't they in every situation made sure we smiled

Why then we can't payback what's due

If parents can handle us so can we too

Let's provide them support and never give reason to cry

Make them understand the unknown rather getting irritated by try

If you're wrong and them being right accept without being shy

They are Gods in flesh brought on earth from sky

Relax, they're old now, they may be irritating at time

But remember the part they played to have you shine

It's said we should treat people as we want to be treated

So behave as you want your children to repeat it.

Setbacks come and will come Again,
Learn from Experiences how to win the game.

Unforeseen situations

When chain of situations make you feel low
Despite you having no reason to bow

When the crops you reaped can't be sowed
When all previous efforts are in dilapidated mode

When you can't help but feel sad
When events force you to go mad

When there's nothing left to fall back on
When even heart is thinking whether to say move-on

When you try but can't turn situation around
When fate ensures tears flow in abound

Then lie on your back or curl on bed
It's ok to cry and feel sad

Give yourself time and keep lying
Then recall all bad which had happened by that time

Try to find what went wrong in situations
Ponder if alternate steps could have avoided complications

Likewise try to find lessons from past occurrence
Store them in mind as an insurance

Jot down the lessons in your notes
Visit them frequently, make them your life quotes
So that similar situations won't again let you down
Moving thus forces life to have you crowned.

Faith and Practice are two strong ingredients,
For your success to never be Disobedient.

Faith & Practise

The two pillars around which your success revolves
That which causes your failures to dissolve

You can't win big without Faith in God and self
Faith of being able to handle whatever comes on shelf

Faith that it's within to accomplish all you can conceive
Along with faith in some higher power that it'll not deceive

Unnerving faith will force nature to give all you deserve
Next comes another pillar i.e. Practise to serve

You can't just sit and wish muscles to grow
Need is to sweat regularly at gym for worth a show

Keep showing up for the task needed for your dream
Don't let the temptations change the scene

Every practise will get you closer to the goal

It's cumulative effect of all steps for making a tasty roll

Regular practise is another must-have key to convert your chance

If still missed have faith that better music will be played to dance

With strong faith and continuous practise in the direction of your goal

None can prevent from ultimately getting your life on roll

Faith should be with no doubts like the faith of a child

Practise such that while pursuing goals you get wild

Pay heed so that nothing prevents you from doing these

Universe forces will then conspire together to say CHEEEEEESSSSEEE.

Why fall in pit when Alternate path is already laid,
Use Books as an aid to avoid in life any long Shade.

Books

I went around and found many motivational
books on sell

Only to wonder why still the bookstore owner was to yell

Why can't he control anger when there's lots of guidance
what to do

Is it because other events in life were making him blue

But don't he had books to guide him with even that

That makes me wonder overall why is this world so sad

Why we see people around being gloomy

When lots of resources are available to make us less steamy

Why we don't have time to work on ourself

When it can save lot of time for other deeds on shelf

Why don't we try to even look into the cause

Are we afraid or has suffering got us so much engrossed

Why don't we recognize that outer world can't disturb
inner peace

Unless one is weak enough to be tweaked

Go and help yourself by giving the BOOKS a try

You'll solve most of hardships instead of opting to cry

Give them a chance

To make you dance

Some research a lot before coming with a best seller

You'll save years by heeding those teller

Don't waste much time and energy to sail mishappenings

Just give books a try, they'll get you giant wings

Do yourself, loved ones a favor and manage some time

Read relevant books to make your life rhyme.

Life's too luxurious to let Unworthy be admitted,
One looks Best in what's most relished and fitted.

People in life

Most people occupy forcefully the space of your life
Some threaten to leave you and go
Some seem to force you to bow

You talked softly with some
You just said hello to others
But soon they engrossed deeper into your joy-de-vivre

Some of them had poison
With threatening looks some intimidate to throw out of horizon

They weren't what you expected to be
You just treated good the people that eyes see

Seemed they have taken you for leverage
Using time and money like a rejected beverage

And when you gathered courage to bade them bye
They pampered with offers which verily were lie

Like an artificial carrot offered for donkey

We sometimes grave to taste fruits of their tree

To be left later with unsatiated thirst

Understand sooner whom to get rid off before it gets worst

As you have all rights to permit whom to let in

Also to throw uninvited who
have been killing from within

Step ahead, identify all and block them everywhere

Don't make them waste any other second of life

Don't allow them anymore to let mind go haywire

Save yourself from their treason's knife

Smile's been and will always be yours

Only if you keep getting rid of those making you insecure.

Mind can bring Pleasures or Worries,
Taste depends on Hands as we cook curries.

Our Mind

Understand your mind…
Our mind is hardwired for negativity and comfort

It tries to keep us in comfortable situation
Choosing least painful ways leading to instant gratification
Giving much lesser rewards than in alternate situation

It distracts us towards different pleasures
At little setbacks it'll keep telling to adapt alternate measures
And when you start moving on that alternate path
At any setback it'll ask to quit and have different start

This chain will keep moving on and on
Shifting your focus so much here and there
With varied things expecting the dawn
Never finishing even one, thus receiving a negative share

When you start anything it's guided by voice of heart
But then mind tries to empower at every missed dart
Whenever you're offered a heavy discounted cart

It's then your control of mind is tasted

And if you give in, your loss is soon to be expected

Whenever in struggle between mind and heart

It's crucial to pay heed to latter's bark

Our worst enemy is our own mind

It makes us think there are other reasons making us blind

Don't forget that your mind is just another organ in body

Slowly-slowly like an exercised muscle it has become rowdy

Still you're in control and not the other way around

Need not to always pay heed to it's tempting sound

You can still own your ground

Being Late is better than never identifying the hound

Force self to listen what heart says

Ensure that all actions to your dreams are obeyed

Have your reasons powerful and
always keep them in sight

Revolt against your mind, show it your might.

Choice's been and will always be Yours,
To stand tall or wreck in Woes.

The Choice

Life is a roller coaster ride
You might have to taste diverse bite
But no matter how longer the tide
Adequately choose not to be bowed by adverse side

Choose never to be lame
To rise despite falling again
To be optimistic despite facing setbacks
To take charge despite all mishaps

Choose to stand strong despite being bowed down
To spread smiles despite being frowned upon
To have faith despite being unlucky
To care despite being bullied

Choose to help despite getting rejections
To love despite receiving least affections
To respect despite being mocked at
To be help-ready despite being flat

Choose to try again to make best use of ticks of clock
To show people a clear passage despite facing blocks

Choose to create a master despite being victimized
To find measures to not let demotivation aggrandize

Choose to give company despite being left alone
To laugh despite having every reason to mourn
To not let anyone affect your choice
To accept ungrudgingly the outcome of your dice
To keep trying to bring desiring days
To not rely on shortcuts or false ways

Choose to ensure you're second to none
Choose to not rest until you're done.

Forgive but don't Forget,
Be cautious to Not regret.

Forgive, Don't Forget

Don't linger on past let it be gone
Thinking about it isn't gonna sharpen the prong

Forgiveness is virtue of the brave
Forget what situations in your life gave

Don't be a victim of circumstances
Don't let them forever devoid you of chances

Lingering on past isn't gonna do any good
This world would have been happier if it could

Jealousy is a weak emotion
Hatred is what gets nothing done

Past failure don't ensure no winning in future
Move on, your new start will heal the sutures

Forgive past fights, losses and all happenings

Use the lessons to make grand endings

Don't forget so that same mistakes aren't repeated again

That's crucial for future steps to not be in vain

Unfavorable past has entangled your lots of energy within

Release them to be used in any productive thing

You'll then do self and loved ones a favor

Increasing productivity, it'll act as a savor.

Your company makes or breaks Growth,
Choose good not bad, neither Both.

Companionship

Beware of your company
i.e. those who often stays in touch

If good they can take to heights
If bad you'll end up getting everywhere denied

If positive it can help you to leave mark
If negative will ensure your capabilities stay in dark

If high spirited you never have to repent
If commonplace it'll create in your smile a dent

If you're enthusiastic about your dream
If you want to be in the cream
Then it's urgent to sort your life's team

They should motivate when you try to be lean
Encouragement should keep coming when you're chasing a dream

Keep them less but none be mean
They'll help to brighten your dull beam

When fruits of your results aren't clear
When you can't see solution any near
When you are hard hit and want to quit
Talk to them, start with a little bit
It's then comes in handy a good company kit

If their being around makes you grow
If they can brighten your life when sun is low
If they help to break your limits
If they just try to suppress your critics
If your back is strong with their support
Always be available for their escort
It doesn't matter if they need to be lured
Such a company is a blessing for sure

If however they make fun of your fails
If you overhear them mocking your tales
If they demotivate you while crossing limit
If they tutor you to be gimmick
If they can't be found in times of need

If they are there due to some greed
If they know to get but don't know to give
If they keep complaining and can't forgive
If you feel sober when they're around
If your many attempts can't change them in any amount
It's better to stay alone than be with such people
If you want to break chain of failure's sequel
With such people however hard you try
Your far less potential is with what you have to satisfy

If however such people are unavoidable
Treat them like an ignored food on table
Let their words flow past you like an air
Though at times they may sound or look fair
But letting them not influence you a bit is in your favor
Then only you get to taste life's palatable savor.

Just Do It, make it Happen,
On practise even One hand can do clapping.

Just do it

Stop just dreaming

Stop waiting, worrying, wondering, contemplating

Stop mumbling, grumbling, hesitating, wishing, frustrating

Stop yourself from disintegrating

Start it living

Steps don't come by chance

Unless you start to dance

You need to jump into the ring to fight

Else you'll keep wondering of other's might

None has reached anywhere just by seeing

You need to start acting than just believing

There is no substitute to start doing it

The football goal needs a hit

Success doesn’t come watching a juggler
Luck comes stuck on back of struggler
There isn’t escaping from this prick
There's no escaping this by any trick

Wishes alone don’t come true
Unless action is the main character of the crew

It's better to be sick doing the thing you want
Rather than fall ill later when repent is on haunt

Enough has been the wait
Time has come to grab the victory’s taste.

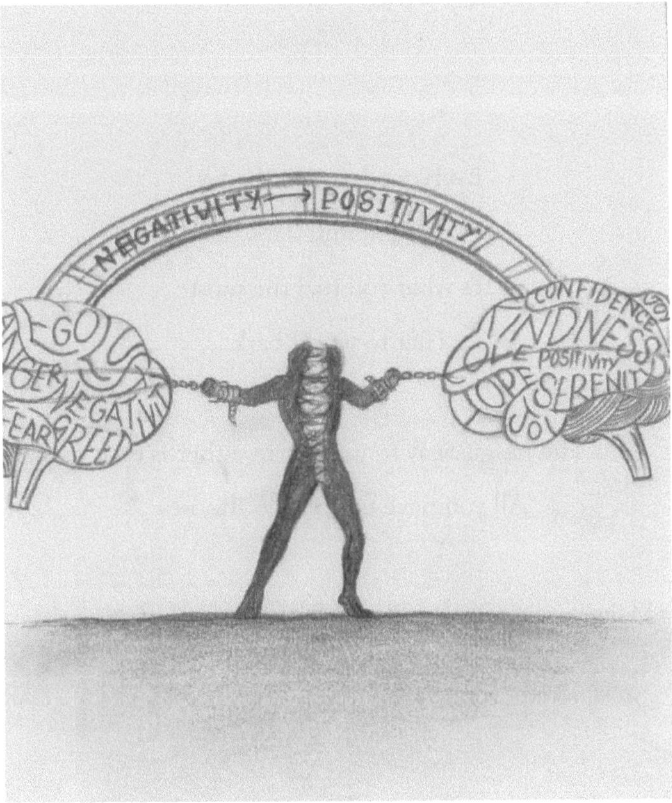

There ain't just one side of coin,

Nor are the two sides Same,

But winning side is One in toss game.

A bridge

Everyone has two shades

Bright and dark

It's what you fuel the most

That to world bark

The passageway to wander in either is easy

All you have to do is be choosey

Make sure you keep filling fuel in the tank that's right

As darkness can't be omitted but can
be suppressed by bright

To suppress your bad first need is to be aware of them

Next is decision to fix it there and then

An active step in this direction is very much required

As just passive wondering will have your life hay-wired

Decide and convert your bad into good soon

Your presence will then be felt like a boon

Do now which most wish later
to had set right

It's urgent necessity to have dark replaced with bright

Though the bridge to travel is difficult to find

But when once found keep transferring files to make your
life shine.

Love ain't easy but it's worth All try,
Ask the starving if he don't Cry.

Love Relationship

Let's list few things which lets love relationship shine
Things which let the two cheers on wine
Respect, Trust, Honesty and Space
These will roll your Love life at a good pace

Respect is the first thing in the list
Without which you'll always feel something's missed
Respect for your partner's present and dreams
Enjoy similarities yet respect your different themes
Respect other's privacy and need for space
Self-respect of either also needs to be embraced

Trusting each other is necessary for love's fulfilment
Building trust requires mutual commitment
Keep proving that you're reliable, responsible and dependable
Saying what you mean and meaning what you say is non-negotiable

Lovers put honesty among top priority
It takes courage to sustain this quality

As truth and feeling's share is its important aspect

A deep sense of security is its effect

Honesty isn't a license to be hurtful or mean

It's a process that needs time, love, and nurturing

Balancing togetherness and space is worth a try

Nourishment and more excitement then qualify

Partners need sense of independence outside of relationship

A single person can't give all sources of joy - a crucial tip

Devote lone time for things that makes you feel great

Also suggest your partner to take this step

Small doses of compromise is needed in healthy relations

Try for negotiations rather than subtractions

Decide on your priorities and let the other hear

Consider it strongly before marrying each other

Active communication gets future roads clear

Misunderstandings needs to be checked from acquiring feather

It takes years to build a good relation

So keep nourishing it to survive in all seasons.

Once you learn to Manage stress,
Every obstacle to Dream seems less.

Stress management

Damn hard this thing is
But it's too costly to be given a miss
As it's important to bring in world sheer bliss
To make life give you a kiss
To decrease regret-later cycle
To provide positivity and energetic survival
To climb success ladder however small
To take control of life overall

We panic in certain situations
Resulting in choosing false directions
Bringing us new complications
Later resulting in lots of frustrations
Of not choosing the alternate path
Of desiring for another start
Of doing what shouldn't be done
Of again letting hopelessness burn
Of failing to stand up to own expectation
Of no growth in handling similar situation

Degrading health and relationships

It also adversely affects one's workmanship

If you can't handle something look for change

If you can't change then expand your range

Stress is crucial to be managed in time

It's been and will be very fine line

To either give in pressure or play what's desired

To control peace from getting hay-wired

Pay heed to your breathing cycle

At instance of stress notice it getting disturbed

Quickly change your location, stay idle

Slow walking and deep breathing is then to be served

Adequate homework needs to be done to handle unexpected case

Relaxation techniques and physical exercises does help you face

Stop to live in a victim's mindset

Fail but important is to learn and next time correct

Be cautious of your self-feedback, it's very important
Unless they're positive, stressful days won't shorten

Negative self-image creates a cycle of feeling low
Avoid those who're happy when you don't grow

Learn to manage anxiety
Learn to handle scarcity

Learn to choose best in the moment
Learn to balance personal and professional endowment

Always prefer supportive ambience to alleviate your mood
Take things positively and practise gratitude

It's important that stress don't let you bow
Will happen only if coping progress continues to grow.

Value things, places, people Nearby;
Trust inner self, it's God's eye.

Valuing nearby

Don't ignore the beauty that's near
It may be faded initially but soon gets clear

Watch closely, it may stand to be brilliant
Like an encapsulated ray which was indeed much radiant
It's like looking in the town for that child
While within our house someone's had it bind

Outside search gets us so much engrossed
That we end up feeling lost
Often our search ends in vain
And we're confused, frustrated or doomed in pain

Exposure to this world teaches us a lot
It did help to untie some of the knots

No doubt this world is surprising, enriching and shining
But inner self and nearby is no less enticing
The best comes when it's cared for and nurtured

It's from inside that some important
questions are answered

Often things and people near us are the best bet
They prove to be more valuable than those far yet

Just coz it's near and easily accessible
Doesn't mean it's less valuable
Start finding value in what's near
Turnouts in life will then be magical.

It's when others think it's The End,
He's still Moving;
It's when people feel Lost,
He's still Pondering;
It's when others yearn to Stop,
Entrepreneur is still Struggling.

Life of an entrepreneur

It ain't about sleepless nights and tiring days
It's rather about doing what heart says...

It isn't about any greed
It's determined NO to join commoner's creed

It's a race to move in light from dark
It's self-promise to leave a mark

It's the craze for living on purpose
It's being the ring master of own circus

It's the love for risk
It's to decide own pace of brisk

It's finding one's true potentials
It's writing our new credentials

It's chasing hope when failures seem to surround
It's creating great charisma when around

It's heeding to our inner voice
It's opting for no compromise

It's mixing days and night as sugar in curd
It's tasting adrenaline shot on accomplishments as dessert

It's being cautious on design every ounce
It's learning new ways for our sales to bounce

It's the fight to outsmart and be creative
It's to see future being imaginative

It's to keep leisure at bay
It's to make sure talents receive at par the pay

It's being stronger after every defeat
It's to keep finding what makes complete

It's passionate never ending toil
It's to be consistent in burning night oil

It's the desire to have what's not
It's to awestruck who thought me a blot

It's to achieve mastery over mind

It's to spread like a melodious chime

It's to grind self to find new flavor

It's to close final eyes with savor.

Love self & bring Joy,
Get confidence & have sorrow Destroyed.

Self-esteem

High self-esteem is too important to be given a miss

Your life needs it to be a bliss

How you feel about yourself is an important aspect

It's a check on how much external sources effect

You might be wrong but important is to recognize right

You might be at loss but necessary is to
take winning stride

Take that leap to jump out from your faults

Don't lie there thinking you're meant to be small

Do self assessment followed by self improvement

Work hard on your shortcomings like you're being given a
punishment

Step by step you can achieve a high self esteem

The building can't sustain itself
unless there's strong beam

You're human so it's ok to fail

Try that only positive self talk decorates your shelf

'You're enough': note that down as slogan

Say it daily to embed in mind as if frozen

Self confidence and self esteem are what's back to back

Stop thinking about failures and keep feeling bad

Don't mistake it with arrogance and haughtiness

It's just that your confidence at any
instance shouldn't be less

Self esteem doesn't mean being selfish and putting self first

It's that negative comments shouldn't let
your confidence burst

Know that it's within you to achieve all that you want

Focus at building confidence will never let you grunt

Identify your gaps and work on them

It's the best investment for making life A GEM

Such people stand out from crowd
and are craved for by others

Personally and professionally
they sail high as if with feathers.

Value what you Got to get value in Life.

For granted

Start valuing what you got before it's too late

We often take people loving us for granted

Busy pleasing those who leave us disenchanted

Often ties with parents, lover and friends are broken because of it

Don't they come first when needed as a handy kit

Ask who don't have them for their importance

When spring goes we do miss it's fragrance

Is there any sense to forget those we are living for

Only to repent later having walked the wrong door

Humans think to have much time on this earth

Wasting it in ignorance never realizing time's true worth

Who's dying can trade any amount for adding seconds

But when alive why don't time has same essence?

Many precious possessions like nature are obtained easily
Taken for granted, such are wasted uselessly
Making us repent outrageously

What's done is done, start cherishing now
Your possessions are priceless somehow

Don't take for granted what's worth much more
Respect your possessions to reach happily life's shore.

If it won't matter Later,
It shouldn't bother Now.

Argument

Relax, calm down

You are shaking from up to down

Your breadth is running fast

You can't think anything except feeling aghast

Can't do anything though you want to get out fast

Will not go if you keep thinking
about the argument's cast

Watch... your mind is full of thoughts of revenge

But don't do anything which you later had to repent

People will try to pull you down

You'll be trapped if you'll try to level their sound

All they want is to lower your standards

Fuck them off... don't be a servant to their orders

If it won't matter in 3 years don't waste even 3 minutes of your time

It's better not to walk than towards a lost shine

Rather than trying to prove yourself right

Let them have false acclamation
while victory's on your side

It ain't worth to compete such reckless who can't ever achieve any height.

So, calm down....relax... take it as a hard test to make you more might

For dreams Wake up,
Work hard, Keep showing up.

Sleeplessness

Why can't I sleep......

Is it because of dreams unfulfilled

Or is it because of being alone

Am I too tired thinking about the wrong

Or done am I trying to find why am born

Can I ever get what's missed to qualify as my home?

Or should I accept the mediocrity and my limits life has shown

Shouldn't I try to challenge myself again

Or be pacified thinking I've whatever I could gain

Should I see those less successful to pacify my pain

Or again start fresh without being insane

Thoughts went all night I couldn't sleep

Even tears seemed dried as I tried to weep

I wondered : Isn't this the one Life I got

Why should I miss any shot

Is lamenting gonna do any good

Is yearning gonna bring desired food?

I've tired, I've failed, I've lost but I'm still alive

Isn't my parents there who love me a lot

What else boost needed than being alive with good health in stock

Why I need others to shower love than those who gave me birth

Who said I can't attain my truc worth?

Who said I can't win after life's done showing me low

Let's face the fact-'It's our set limits before which we bow'

As a child we never doubted to win next regardless of how much we lost

Then why not again try to spread
cheese properly on toast

Why not start to again bake the cake

I woke up that mid-night to try another chance at fate.

Less important kills Much time,
With little left for Important to rhyme.

Priorities

Learn to set priorities in life
Else you'll have lesser time for what you should strive

Lean time shouldn't go in haste
Invest to soon have your goal's taste

Lots of dishes comprise a buffet
But delicious meals often keep nutrition at bay

Instant pleasures are like being on path with many pitfall
Why thus make it tough to reach desired stall

Batsman observes every ball to knows what's worth a hit
Don't be tempted by lots of glittering kit

Stop ignoring guidance from your inner sound
Nobody is posting any of their wound

Social media is making you anti-social,
hypocrite and depressed

It's hard to find a not-fake jewel's chest

Prioritize deeds according to their importance

Let urgent things be first given chance

Watch clock at intervals, pay heed to time to tasks

There's so much to do with important often buried in flask

80-20 work-leisure ratio gets often reversed

Leisure is like a ransom paid to let failure be served

Today so much of trivial things compete for our attention

That only a strict schedule can move us in goal's direction

Go through your goals often,
let them be engrossed in mind

5 minutes for priority list each day will control emphasiz

Don't let others force you to prioritize

Sit over unexpected events to decide
what's to emphasize

Goodness to society or to others in real need
should also be taken up

Unworthy tasks shouldn’t be allowed to crowd your stuff

Make sure to keep track of priorities' progress thrice after
meals in a day

To sail life's journey being satisfied and gay.

Start to lead, enough Followed,
Relevant habits should be Swallowed.

The follower

Wait.. relax.. take another thought...
Why are you busy following the crowd

Why can't you take a stand
Are you afraid of being left out or of your can't

Why do you need to do what they have done
Why need is to backstab to go in front

Why can't you stand against organizational culture
Are you afraid to take loneliness torture?

Why you chose to ignore new and follow what's done
Though you know it's wrong and did know some
Who have gone their way and known for what they become
Still why are you afraid to heed those some

Who's stopping to not follow what's wrong

Why can't you play own virtuous song

It's infectious to follow the crowd

Gossip will let your qualities drain out

Your talents will soon vanish from mind

Backstage will leave you behind

Realization will be far later of wasting your chance

As while talent was hacked you and
job-security were on romance

Left only to repent for flowing with the wind

As by then the path to return had been too thinned

Your talents will rust you'll not die in peace

Your life is not from someone on lease

Is job security really worth to trade your dreams for

Isn't there limited validity to taste
sweet before it turns sour

If you want to be happy and shine

If you want sleep to taste like precious wine

Choose being a boss and not a clerk
There's dearth of talent, there's audience for your worth

Start to play your tunes on harp
Stop joining the dog's bark

Stop following to increase followers
Start building your own, stop being a borrower

You're on a purpose, don't carry as it is to grave
You're here to shine, decorate own path, be brave

Your voice should stand out from the rest
Who knows maybe you could turn to be the BEST

It's better to start moving when still alive and can refresh
Than wishing when diseases and/or old age enmesh.

Victory in life is in All roles,
Serve each to be a Blessed soul.

Roles of life

We all have many roles to play

Sacrificing one for another can't keep you gay

Make sure to balance and prioritize each

Such that important isn't far from reach

A winner ain't praised by society
but not loved by in nest

Real winner is one living all roles of life to best

Trees of different lengths breadths
make for a perfect view

Living all roles is what makes life worth a show

Winning one to extreme and losing
another calls for tragic end

None for sure keeps same speed on bend

Varying speed is what adds in a successful trip

Varying colors is what makes a beautiful click

You can't just stand and wait for fewer
vehicles to be on road

How then a single win makes you to gloat

Be a winner also in parent's, better half's and
your children's eye

Learn to be looked upon not by crowd but by sky

Do fulfill relationship and society
goals besides money ones

Aspire to be a better human being to forever stay happy
and young.

Pressure ain't Always positive,
Managing it makes life Progressive.

Manage the pressure

True performance germinate when voices force down
When there's milliseconds to face the hound
When you can't sit over pros cons rather have to show your game
Preparation helps savvy what's across blurred aim

We all are blessed with God's clue
Take deep breaths let that inner sound guide you
Ask questions, clarify for fast reply shouldn't pervert you

It's your right to say no
if you think the need is so

Don't give in to pressure, a poisonous thorn
Handle with care the sharp corn

People bypass thinking in lure of cents
Heeding to inner voice lets safely cross the fence

Afraid of consequences?
Ahhh.... inner voice is never wrong
But listening to it ain't handy

We often ignore it as uselessly pricky
You need to practice to start giving it a kiss
It's too precious to be given a miss.

Run for they have Already walked,

Don't stop for Victory's door waits
Unknocked.

Run

Your time has now come to throw open all gates
Right time is now to jump in the race
Doesn't matter how far the rest have travelled
To handle downs, life's job is to get you more braced

Others might not yet be lustrous enough to shine
They might be far from finishing line
Possibly they might have suffered breakdown
Finishing ribbon might still be intact for thine

There's no right time to start
There's no right place for lark
Once you set it in mind
Get deaf to intriguing bark

Everyone has their own clock
Everyone has to look after their stock
Everyone has their share of low
Get key to cause of unfavorable past lock
When you realize 'It's time' starts your day

Till then day's brightness equals dark night

It's on pursuing urgently your say

That darkest tunnel illuminates brighter than past's daylight.

From feeding with Food, Air & Life lesson,
None exist without Nature's affection,
Stay in harmony for nature's Gift's reception.

Environment

Don't be so obsessed with yourself
That you forget owe to this world
You're being fed and bred by this society
Try listening to the screams hurled

Don't ignore elders, beggars and the wounded
For we're in relationship with all surrounded
As we share same air with animals and plants
Contribute to ecosystem also by choice not only by chance

Spend a little less at partying and shopping
Collective small savings can bring changes whopping

Enough been taking, learn the art of giving
Returns ain't immediate but huge be while living

Being the source of light, life and nutrition
No detailing's enough for nature's gift's definition
From being life guide to bestowing with many medicine
Nature's innumerable offerings has least in return seen

The exploitation has been to such great extent

That regenerative capacity is beyond any expense

Urgent need is cautiousness & many front-foots to save

To prevent next generation from
reaching sooner the grave

Add environmental conservation and social service part of
calendar

Health and happiness will be the reward for
services rendered

Universe traces and never forgets to pay such souls

Respect nature to be healthy thus wealthy and have peace
in control.

Not less Not much just Needed attention,
Brings in life much needed Satisfaction.

Attention

Give only that much attention as is deserved
It tastes good only with requisite amount served

Often we're clogged up in abundant attention cage
Be it towards some person, thing, topic or rage
Letting the outcome to vary from our page

Learn timely to be a sage
Prune your screenplay onstage

Even movies have diverse cast
If improperly balanced, collections won't last

Learning to allot adequate attention isn't smooth
Only when life's suffocating do we get the truth

Test is...
If important things cry for your time,
If near and dear ones need to stand in line
Stop to ask, "Is everything's fine?"
Introspect then for what is but shouldn't be prime
Not all attention seekers need be attention grabbers
Adequate ingredients keep tasty for long before turning
slime.

Often a born Winner is duped by Life to be a Loser
Grabbing adequate Opportunity in Time can still crown you Sir

Lion's story

The lioness was hunted down by poachers. Her cub, a lion was hungry and for first time there was no one to feed him.

Never been before on hunt all by himself he, however, was determined to satisfy his hunger, so he went in wild. For entire day he couldn't find anything to feed himself, the sole reason being that he didn't tried hard enough. Often he chose the path with less thorns out of fear of being injured.

Filled with frustration he was sitting under a tree when a group of wolfs surrounded him. They offered him a piece of flesh to satisfy his hunger which was much less with respect to his diet but he accepted thanking for the little he was offered.

He joined the wolf's group with a deal that he be roaring and leading when asked to do so in return for getting the food.

Though often sleeping with half filled stomach, at times he thought of escaping from that group but then with the almost free lunch and the little labour he was asked to do, a sense of false gratification and laziness crept in.

Another reason of why he didn't tried hard enough to get out was because he met few in that group who looked like lion as himself. Slowly, as time passed by, his mindset became similar to other wolfs and he one among them.

Then, one day, he witnessed another lion, Shera, in his forest who was said to have escaped from another forest since some days. He was very much impressed by stories of Shera and of his might.

On one such encounter Shera spoke with him, adequate attention was then paid to his words. That day when he went back to his wolf's group he found that whom he thought to be lions in that group were actually wolfs in lion's clothing.

He slowly started getting suffocated. He wanted to follow Shera, who seem to remind him of his true capabilities. Now he started to try not to fit in but to find his real self.

Again there wasn't much effort being put by him but he then knew that he was not born to die out of depression. He knew he can feed all his desires. He knew he too can be powerful. He then knew he was born to rule and not being ruled.

But all this was possible only if he start to prepare for his escape which will not be easy as he has forgotten all his capabilities and has become at par with wolfs .

Moreover, wolfs will try all tricks to make sure he can't leave as he was an asset for them. But then cub was grown up and wolfs couldn't fool him anymore. He knew that it's been enough and time has come to prepare for a final escape.

He thought it to be better to try and fail and then try again rather than die with regret as he was continuously reminded of his strengths, of his role in society, of his capabilities, of his dreams and of being a ruler.

And now he Is determined to be LION again.

Author bio

The author is an engineer by profession, a designer, an influencer and a writer by hobby who is on a mission to make this world a happy place to live in with the impact of powerful weapon called words.

Just an average guy always trying for not so average task of motivating people around and also showing how little changes in our life can bring whooping changes in our happiness quotient. He aspires for a world where people are with smiles, where people live their life extraordinarily utilizing every moment, creating memories with zero regrets.

This book has been his life guide to travel from every setback to comeback and is now available for the world to try tested recipe for being the master of own life and living our dreams.

Let's START LIVING.....

9 789393 809766

Printed by Libri Plureos GmbH in Hamburg, Germany